Encounters with God

The Gospel of MATTHEW

Encounters with God Study Guide Series

Encounters with God

The Gospel of MATTHEW

Published by Thomas Nelson, Inc., P.O. Box 141000, Nashville, Tennessee 37214.

Scripture quotations are taken from The New King James Version® (NKJV), copyright 1979, 1980, 1982, 1992 Thomas Nelson, Inc., Publishers.

Library of Congress Cataloging-in-Publication Data
ISBN 1-4185-14209

Printed in the United States of America

07 08 09 10 RRD 9 8 7 6 5 4 3 2 1

CONTENTS

AN INTRODUCTION TO THE GOSPEL OF MATTHEW

The Gospel of Matthew is more than just the first book of the New Testament—in many ways, it is the bridge between the Old and New Testaments. It is a book that is decidedly Jewish and decidedly Christian, simultaneously.

A Gospel Account. At the outset of this study, we should consider several general terms often applied to this New Testament book. Matthew is a gospel account—one of four books in the New Testament labeled *Gospels*. It joins Mark, Luke, and John as a book that is all about Jesus—what He did, what He said, and who He was and is. The word *gospel* literally means *good news*. Matthew was writing to tell the good news of Jesus' miraculous and miracle-filled life, His life-giving messages, His sacrificial and atoning death, and His hope-inspiring and divine resurrection from the dead. The life, death, and resurrection of Jesus are certainly the greatest news that has ever been proclaimed from heaven to earth. It is the heart of the gospel message through the ages. It is a living message that extends from Jesus' first-century life to this present moment.

A Synoptic Gospel. Matthew is considered to be a *synoptic* Gospel, along with the Gospel accounts of Mark and Luke. The word synoptic means *seeing from one viewpoint* or *one overview*. Matthew, Mark, and Luke cover many of the same incidents and messages of Jesus in their Gospel accounts. In many ways, their accounts are similar to three photograph albums taken by three different photographers covering essentially the same life and events. Just as each photographer has a unique vantage point, angle, and composition, so each of the synoptic Gospels has a distinct voice, style, and purpose. Each Gospel account covers some events and messages that aren't recorded by the others. The events or messages presented are covered with differing degrees of depth and breadth. But in general, each of the synoptic Gospels presents an overview of the life, death, and resurrection of Jesus.

Where the synoptic Gospel writers differ the most is in their audience, and therefore, the purpose for what they say and how they say it. Mark wrote his Gospel account primarily for Roman believers in Jesus Christ. Luke wrote his Gospel account to one person in leadership. Matthew wrote His Gospel primarily for Jewish believers. The Gospel of Matthew is decidedly the most Jewish of the New Testament Gospels.

Matthew's purpose was to assure his Jewish readers that Jesus was God's Son and the long-awaited Messiah foretold by the Old Testament prophets. The Gospel presents Jesus as the fulfillment of Israel's prophetic hope— Matthew is the Gospel writer who specifically tells how Jesus fulfilled Old Testament prophecies related to His birth (1:22–23), birthplace (2:5–6), return from Egypt (2:15), residence in Nazareth (2:23), having a messianic forerunner (3:1–3), location of His public ministry (4:14–16), healing ministry (8:14–17), role as God's servant (12:17–21), teaching in parables (13:34–35), triumphant entry into Jerusalem (21:4–5), and arrest (26:56). Matthew did not limit himself to Jewish concerns, but his message is aimed primarily at a Jewish audience and he therefore is very sensitive to those aspects of Jesus' life that will fulfill messianic claims.

Matthew tells us several things about Jesus that the other Gospel writers do not emphasize or mention, and those are what we focus on in this study guide: the visit of the magi, the temptation in the wilderness, the message we call the Sermon on the Mount, and the emphasis on what it means to experience the kingdom of heaven on this earth.

Matthew the Author. Two facts about Matthew as a Gospel writer are useful to consider. First, he was an eyewitness to the life of Jesus. The church has agreed from earliest recorded documents that Matthew was one of the twelve disciples closely associated with Jesus. (Neither Mark nor Luke were among the apostles.) Second, Matthew was a tax collector prior to his following Jesus. He had an accountant's mind—he wrote with precision, systematic order, and logic. From the earliest centuries, the church relied heavily upon the Gospel of Matthew to instruct new converts.

AN OVERVIEW OF OUR STUDY
OF THE GOSPEL OF MATTHEW

This study guide presents seven lessons drawn from and based largely on the Gospel of Matthew. The study guide elaborates on, and is based on, the commentary included in the *Blackaby Study Bible*. The lessons are:

Lesson #1: Jesus Is King!

Lesson #2: Jesus Overcame the Tempter

Lesson #3: Jesus Taught How to Live a Blessed Life

Lesson #4: Jesus Emphasized the Inner Life and the Law of Love

Lesson #5: Jesus Taught His Followers How to Pray

Lesson #6: Jesus Taught in Parables

Lesson #7: Jesus Taught about Kingdom Living

Personal or Group Use. These lessons are offered for personal study and reflection or for small-group Bible study. The questions may be answered by an individual reader or used as a foundation for group discussion. A section titled "Notes to Leaders of Small Groups" is included at the back of this book to help those who might lead a group study of the material.

Before you embark on this study, we encourage you to read in full "How to Study the Bible" in the *Blackaby Study Bible* on pages viii–ix. Our contention is always that the Bible is unique among all literature. It is God's definitive word for humanity. The Bible is:

- *inspired*—God breathed

- *authoritative*—absolutely the final word on any spiritual matter

- *the plumb line of truth*—the standard against which all human activity and reasoning must be evaluated

The Bible is fascinating in that it has remarkable diversity, but also remarkable unity. The books were penned by a diverse assortment of authors representing a variety of languages and cultures. The Bible as a whole has a number of literary forms. But, the Bible's message from cover to cover is clear, consistent, and unified.

More than mere words on a page, the Bible is an encounter with God Himself. No book is more critical to your life. The very essence of the Bible is the Lord Himself.

God speaks by the Holy Spirit through the Bible. He also communicates during your time of prayer, in your life circumstances, and through the church. Read your Bible in an attitude of prayer and allow the Holy Spirit to make you aware of God's activity in and through your personal life. Write down what you learn, meditate on it, and adjust your thoughts, attitudes, and behavior accordingly. Look for ways every day in which the truth of God's Word can be applied to your circumstances and relationships. God is not random, but orderly and intentional in the way He speaks to you.

Be encouraged—the Bible is *not* too difficult for the average person to understand if that person asks the Holy Spirit for help. (Furthermore, not even the most brilliant person can fully understand the Bible apart from the Holy Spirit's help!) God desires for you to know Him and His Word. Everyone who reads the Bible can learn from it. The person who will receive maximum benefit from reading and studying the Bible, however, is the one who:

- *is born again* (John 3:3, 5). Those who are born again and have received the gift of God's Spirit have a distinct advantage in understanding the deeper truths of His Word.

- *has a heart that desires to learn God's truth.* Your attitude greatly influences the outcome of Bible study. Resist the temptation to focus on what others have said about the Bible. Allow the Holy Spirit to guide you as you study God's Word for yourself.

- *has a heart that seeks to obey God.* The Holy Spirit teaches most those who have a desire to apply what they learn. Begin your Bible study with prayer, asking the Holy Spirit to guide your thoughts and to impress on you what is on God's heart. Then, make plans to adjust your life immediately to obey the Lord fully.

As you read and study the Bible, your purpose is not to *create* meaning, but to *discover* the meaning of the text with the Holy Spirit's guidance. Ask yourself, "What did the author have in mind? How was this applied by those who first heard these words?" Especially in your study of the Gospel accounts, pay attention to the words of Jesus that begin, "Most assuredly" or "He opened His mouth and taught them, saying." These are core principles and teachings that powerfully impact every person's life.

At times you may find it helpful to consult other passages of the Bible (made available in the center columns in the *Blackaby Study Bible*) or the commentary in the margins of the *Blackaby Study Bible*.

Keep in mind always that Bible study is not primarily an exercise for acquiring information, but it is an opportunity for transformation. Bible study is your opportunity to encounter God and to be changed in His presence. When God speaks to your heart, nothing remains the same. Jesus said, "He who has ears to hear, let him hear" (Matthew 13:9). Choose to have ears that desire to hear!

The B-A-S-I-Cs of Each Study in This Guide. Each lesson in this study guide has five segments, using the word BASIC as an acronym. The word BASIC does not allude to elementary or simple, but rather, to *foundational*. These studies extend the concepts that are part of the *Blackaby Study Bible* commentary and are focused on key aspects of what it means to be a Christ-follower in today's world. The BASIC acronym stands for:

B = *Bible Focus*. This segment presents the central passage for the lesson and a general explanation that covers the central theme or concern.

A = *Application for Today*. This segment has a story or illustration related to modern-day times, with questions that link the Bible text to today's issues, problems, and concerns.

S = *Supplementary Scriptures to Consider*. In this segment, other Bible verses related to the general theme of the lesson are explored.

I = *Introspection and Implications*. In this segment, questions are asked that lead to deeper reflection about one's personal faith journey and life experiences.

C = *Communicating the Good News*. This segment presents challenging questions aimed at ways in which the truth of the lesson might be lived out and shared with others (either to win the lost or build up the church).

LESSON #1

JESUS IS KING!

Messiah: Savior, liberator
Christ: Greek for "Savior," "Messiah"
King: Ruler of a people, one who establishes
and maintains a kingdom

B
Bible Focus

> The book of the genealogy of Jesus Christ, the Son of David, the Son of Abraham: . . . and Jesse begot David the king. . . . So all the generations from Abraham to David are fourteen generations, from David until the captivity in Babylon are fourteen generations, and from the captivity in Babylon until the Christ are fourteen generations (Matthew 1:1, 6, 17).
>
> Now after Jesus was born in Bethlehem of Judea in the days of Herod the king, behold, wise men from the East came to Jerusalem, saying, "Where is He who has been born King of the Jews? For we have seen His star in the East and have come to worship Him." . . . And when they had come into the house, they saw the young Child with Mary His mother, and fell down and worshiped Him. And when they had opened their treasures, they presented gifts to Him: gold, frankincense, and myrrh (Matthew 2:1–2, 11).
>
> In those days John the Baptist came preaching in the wilderness of Judea, and saying, "Repent, for the kingdom of heaven is at hand!" . . . Then Jerusalem, all Judea, and all the region around the Jordan went out to him and were baptized by him in the Jordan, confessing their sins. But when he saw many of the Pharisees and Sadducees coming to his baptism, he said to them. . . . "I indeed baptize you with water unto repentance, but He who is coming after me is mightier than I, whose sandals I am not worthy to carry. He will baptize you with the Holy Spirit and fire." . . . Then Jesus came from Galilee to John at the Jordan to be baptized by him. And John tried to prevent Him, saying, "I need to be baptized by You, and are You coming to me?" But Jesus answered and said to him, "Permit it to be so now, for thus it is fitting for us to fulfill all righteousness." Then he allowed Him. When He had been baptized, Jesus came up immediately from the water; and behold, the heavens were opened to Him, and He saw the Spirit of God descending like a dove and alighting upon Him. And suddenly a voice came from heaven, saying, "This is My beloved Son, in whom I am well pleased" (Matthew 3:1, 5–7, 11, 13–17).

One of Matthew's foremost purposes is to establish Jesus as Messiah—the long-awaited, divinely-appointed King of the Jewish people. One of the key

principles in the Jewish tradition is this: out of the mouth of two or three
witnesses, justice and truth are established. (See Deuteronomy 17:6 and
19:15.) This principle carried over into New Testament times. (See
2 Corinthians 13:1.)

Matthew offers three forms of proof—or witness—that Jesus qualifies as
King. He first cites the lineage of Jesus, and he does it in accountant-like
terms. Jesus is shown to be a direct descendant of both Abraham and David.
Jesus is clearly proclaimed to be a Jew, with Abraham—the father of all who
have faith—as both His spiritual and biological ancestor. (See Romans 4:16.)
Jesus is also of the lineage of King David, to whom an everlasting throne was
promised. (See 2 Samuel 7:13 and Isaiah 9:7.) Not only does Jesus fit the
prescribed identity for Messiah, but, according to Matthew, Jesus appears in
history after three sets of fourteen generations—these multiples of seven (in
couplets representing the days of the patriarchs, the kings, and the prophets),
had special numerical meaning to the Jewish people. Six groups of seven have
passed, which puts Jesus at the threshold of the *seventh seven*—a numerical
position of perfect rule, since seven is the biblical number that refers to
perfection in Jewish tradition.

While we as Christians today do not place emphasis on ancestry, bloodline,
or the meaning of numbers as the Jewish people did in the first century, we
can draw a very special meaning from this first chapter of Matthew: Jesus
came *precisely* according to God's perfect timing, with *precisely* the right
natural qualifications to be Messiah. No one but Jesus has ever fit the profile
of being the King of kings, with an everlasting spiritual reign.

The second proof Matthew provides for Jesus being King is the appearance
of magi from afar. These non-Jewish wise men traveled to Jerusalem, and then
on to Bethlehem, with the sole purpose of paying homage to a new king. They
not only bow before the new king, but they present Him with valuable gifts
that are, in retrospect, symbolic of Jesus' messianic role: gold for His king-
ship, frankincense that symbolizes His priestly role, and myrrh that
foreshadows His sacrificial death.

The third witness Matthew provides for Jesus being King flows from the
ministry of John the Baptist, the great prophet of repentance who is to *prepare
the way of the Lord* (Matthew 3:3). John the Baptist was the first nationally
recognized prophet in Israel in nearly four hundred years and his popularity
and effectiveness among the people were tremendous. John clearly identifies
Jesus as the Messiah, one who has all authority to baptize with the Holy Spirit
and to *burn up the chaff with unquenchable fire* (Matthew 3:12)—establishing
a new spiritual order, something only the Messiah was considered qualified to
do. Matthew identifies the fullness of the Trinity as being present at Jesus'
baptism: Jesus the Son emerges from the waters of baptism to see the Holy
Spirit alighting upon Him *like a dove* (Matthew 3:16) and hear the voice of

His heavenly Father proclaiming, *"This is My beloved Son, in whom I am well pleased"* (Matthew 3:17).

Historically and traditionally, culturally and symbolically, spiritually and divinely, Matthew proves Jesus is the King, the Messiah, the Savior!

The tremendous comfort we can have as Christians today is this: God confirms to us in countless ways *our* identity in Christ Jesus. He speaks to us through the natural world; His divinely inspired Word, the Bible; the confirming words of others; and deep within the recesses of our own spirit. He does not just assure us once of His presence, power, provision, and protection, but repeatedly. He speaks to all who have *ears to hear* and *eyes to see*.

A
Application for Today

Every generation of citizens in the United States has had an inflow of immigrants. At times, especially large numbers from a particular nation or region of the world have come to the United States seeking asylum, freedom, or opportunity. "Where are you from?" has been a common question for Americans to ask one another.

The people in Jesus' time asked Him this same question. However, they were seeking an answer to an even deeper question, "Who are you?" These questions are present, if not spoken directly, in the story of the magi coming to worship Jesus. They are questions that those who studied genealogy and those who stood on the banks of the Jordan River no doubt asked about Jesus.

What types of questions do we tend to ask strangers today when it comes to their spiritual identity? "Are you a Christian?" or "What church do you attend?" At times, we ask, "Do you know Jesus Christ as your Savior?" Rarely do we ask one of the most important questions, "Are you following Jesus daily as your Lord?" At issue is our identity in Christ.

Who *are* you in Christ Jesus?

Does your family heritage have any role to play in your spiritual identity? If so, what role? How important is that role, or should that role be?

To what degree do you base your spiritual identity on what others have taught you? On your association with other Christian people? On what someone has prophesied about you?

People in Jesus' time no doubt described Him using a wide variety of terms. What the Gospels reveal to us is not only their opinions and evaluations, but far more importantly, who Jesus said He was and is, and how His deeds confirmed His claims.

How do *you* identity yourself spiritually? On the basis of what facts? To what degree do you struggle with living out your own definition of what it means to be a follower of Christ Jesus?

What happens when someone comes into your circle of acquaintances, saying, "I am a good Christian," but their definition of *Christian* doesn't match up with your definition, or what you believe to be the Bible's definition? What happens when their behavior doesn't line up with what you believe is godly Christlike behavior?

S
Supplementary Scriptures to Consider

The apostle Paul wrote to the Corinthians using these very bold, sobering, and challenging words:

> This will be the third time I am coming to you. *"By the mouth of two or three witnesses every word shall be established."* I have told you before, and foretell as if I were present the second time, and now being absent I write to those who have sinned before, and to all the rest, that if I come again I will not spare—since you seek a proof of Christ speaking in me, who is not weak toward you, but mighty in you. For though He was crucified in weakness, yet He lives by the power of God. For we also are weak in Him, but we shall live with Him by the power of God toward you.
>
> Examine yourselves as to whether you are in the faith. Test yourselves. Do you not know yourselves, that Jesus Christ is in you? (2 Corinthians 13:1–5)

- How important are the affirmations, encouraging words, and instructional words of other godly men and women to your knowing that Jesus Christ is in you?

• What must we do to guard against error and against convincing ourselves and others that we are OK? What is the standard against which we must always judge our own identity in Christ and our behavior?

While it was very important to Matthew to identify Jesus as a Jew who was fully qualified to be the Messiah, the apostle Paul wrote to the early Christian believers in Colossae:

> But now you yourselves . . . have put on the new man who is renewed in knowledge according to the image of Him who created him, where there is neither Greek nor Jew, circumcised nor uncircumcised, barbarian, Scythian, slave nor free, but Christ is all and in all (Colossians 3:8, 10–11).

How difficult is it to overcome racial prejudice, even in the church? To what degree do we tend to align ourselves with people of like race, cultural traditions, and socioeconomic level? What does Christ challenge us to do?

The prophet Isaiah said this about the coming Messiah, a prophecy fulfilled in every way by Jesus Christ:

For unto us a Child is born,
Unto us a Son is given;
And the government will be upon His shoulder.
And His name will be called
Wonderful, Counselor, Mighty God,
Everlasting Father, Prince of Peace.
Of the increase of His government and peace

There will be no end,
Upon the throne of David and over His kingdom
To order it and establish it with judgment and justice.
From that time forward, even forever.
The zeal of the Lord of hosts will perform this
        (Isaiah 9:6–7).

• To what extent have you experienced these attributes of Jesus in accepting Him as your Savior and Lord: Wonderful, Counselor, Mighty God, Everlasting Father, Prince of Peace?

• To what extent, and in what ways, has Jesus' rule over your life and behavior increased since you first accepted Him as your Savior?

• In what ways is the Lord ordering your life and establishing you with increasing judgment and justice?

• The prophet Isaiah described the Messiah as being *Wonderful, Counselor, Mighty God, Everlasting Father,* and *Prince of Peace.* What descriptive words are the foremost words you might use to describe who *you* are as a Christian?

I

Introspection and Implications

1. Do you feel you don't really know who you are in Christ Jesus? How might you begin to make this discovery?

2. Do you have a sense of your own destiny and purpose? If so, can you express it in a single sentence? If not, how might you begin to gain an awareness of what Christ has destined for you on this earth?

3. To what extent do you draw your self-definition from other people? Are there ways in which you need to rely less on the opinions of others? How might you rely more on what the Word of God says about who you are and why you are on this earth? How might you help others, including

your own children, to define themselves according to their relationship with Christ Jesus?

4. The genealogy of Jesus given in the Gospel of Matthew includes four women. Women were typically excluded from genealogies, so this is unusual. Even more unusual is their inclusion because of who they were! Tamar had a scandalous relationship with Judah (Genesis 38), Rahab was a Canaanite harlot from Jericho (Joshua 2), Ruth was a Moabite (Ruth 1:4), and Bathsheba committed adultery with David (2 Samuel 11:1—12:25). Their inclusion reflects God's forgiveness and grace to all people. In your life, are there some ancestors—perhaps even a member of your immediate or extended family today—you would like to disown? Have you ever allowed the bad behavior of a family member to define you? With what result? In what ways does the Lord challenge us to look beyond the past in our life, and the lives of others, and to focus on the forgiveness and grace made possible by Christ Jesus?

5. To what extent is it important to honor the cultural values and heritage of others who come to know Jesus as their Savior? How might these cultural values and heritage be expressed within the church?

6. There is nothing about the physical, outward appearance of Jesus that would have automatically proclaimed to the world in which He lived: "I'm the Messiah." Jesus likely looked Jewish—but so did countless other men in His time. Many people in our world today wear garments, jewelry items, or other identifying marks to signal their religion, but also to signal their status, their roles in society, or their culture. In what ways are outward signs helpful? A hindrance?

C
Communicating the Good News

Matthew proclaims Jesus as the Christ to Jews in his time. What forms of witness or proof would you use to proclaim Jesus as Savior to your world? Challenge yourself! Identify what you consider to be the three main facts that you would share with another person to prove that Jesus is the Savior.

Matthew's proofs about Jesus point to a precision in God's timing, something often called the *fullness of time*. In what ways can you look back on your own acceptance of Jesus as Savior and see precision in the way God worked in your life? In what ways are we challenged to allow God's methods and timing to unfold in another person's life? In what ways are we challenged to recognize that God may be using *us* as one of His methods, and to see *now* as His perfect timing in our expression of the gospel to another person?

LESSON #2

JESUS OVERCAME THE TEMPTER

Temptation: a craving or desire for something contrary to God's commandments—an enticement that draws a person away from God

B
Bible Focus

> *Then Jesus was led up by the Spirit into the wilderness to be tempted by the devil. And when He had fasted forty days and forty nights, afterward He was hungry. Now when the tempter came to Him, he said, "If You are the Son of God, command that these stones become bread."*
>
> *But He answered and said, "It is written, 'Man shall not live by bread alone, but by every word that proceeds from the mouth of God.'"*
>
> *Then the devil took Him up into the holy city, set Him on the pinnacle of the temple, and said to Him, "If You are the Son of God, throw Yourself down. For it is written: 'He shall give His angels charge over you,' and, 'In their hands they shall bear you up, lest you dash your foot against a stone.'"*
>
> *Jesus said to him, "It is written again, 'You shall not tempt the LORD your God."*
>
> *Again the devil took Him up on an exceedingly high mountain, and showed Him all the kingdoms of the world and their glory. And he said to Him, "All these things I will give You if You will fall down and worship me." Then Jesus said to him, "Away with you, Satan! For it is written, 'You shall worship the LORD your God, and Him only you shall serve."*
>
> *Then the devil left Him, and behold, angels came and ministered to Him (Matthew 4:1–11).*

Matthew is the only one of the Gospel writers who gives us details about Jesus' encounter with the devil prior to the start of His earthly ministry.

Four aspects of this passage warrant our close attention. First, Matthew tells us that Jesus *was led up by the Spirit into the wilderness to be tempted by the devil* (Matthew 11:1). God the Father wasn't tempting or testing Jesus. But God was allowing the devil to tempt or test Him. Why? In part, because Jesus was fully human, even as He was fully divine. It was the humanity of Jesus that was being put to the test.

Second, the temptations of the devil play on key facets of behavior common to all human beings. We often call these *drives* or *lusts*. Every human being craves physical satisfaction. We have a hunger drive, a thirst drive, a sex drive, a drive to feel safe and comfortable from the harsh forces of nature. The devil came to Jesus after He had fasted forty days and forty nights and was hungry. The devil tempted Jesus to use His divinity to meet His human need—he tempted Jesus to turn stones into bread.

The devil very often comes to us to tempt us first and foremost to use whatever methods we can to satisfy our fleshly drives.

When that temptation didn't work on Jesus, the devil addressed the human emotional desire we all have for recognition. Every person has a need to feel valuable, worthy, or important. We want others to notice us and appreciate us. The devil offered Jesus an exciting, very visible way to gain attention and notoriety—jump from the corner of the temple into the valley below and let the angels swoop Him miraculously to safety. What a way to headline the start of a miracle ministry! Jesus didn't cave in.

The devil turned to yet a third temptation aimed at basic human pride: the devil offered Jesus influence and power. Every human being to some degree wants to be number one—to be the center of someone's attention and affection, to be the person in charge, to be the one who dictates what is done when and how and where and to what effect. We are self-centered creatures. The devil offered Jesus the opportunity to rule over all the kingdoms of the world.

The devil comes to us with temptations wrapped in these same human drives and desires. He tempts us to compromise what we know to be God's standards to meet our physical needs. He tempts us to seek fame and attention to prove we are noteworthy and worthy to be loved. He tempts us to seek positions of power so we might have our way, not God's way, in all things.

Third, the devil was defeated in each of his temptations by the Word of God. Jesus quoted verses from the book of Deuteronomy to the devil! Jesus used what we each have within our grasp to use in defeating the temptations of the devil—the Word of God spoken with authority and resolve.

Fourth, the devil left Jesus after Jesus said to him, *"Away with you."* Then, and only then, the Gospel of Matthew tells us, *angels came and ministered to Him* (Matthew 11:11). Angels, who by definition are ministers of God, gave to Jesus what He needed in the aftermath of His confrontation with the devil. They no doubt provided physical sustenance for Him. Their very presence no doubt confirmed to Jesus that, indeed, He was surrounded by God's protecting angels. And the angels may very well have reminded Jesus that He already had all power and authority over the kingdoms of the world *as long as* He worshiped His heavenly Father and Him alone.

We can be assured of one overriding truth: God may allow the devil to tempt or test us, but the purpose in the testing is so we will know who we are in Christ Jesus. God fully expects us to use His Word in defeating the devil. God fully expects us to emerge on the other side of temptation refined and prepared more fully for the service He calls us to render to the world.

A
Application for Today

A number of years ago, a prominent person in American society—the First Lady of our nation, Nancy Reagan—was asked what a young person should say if he was offered drugs. Her simple reply became a rallying cry for countless people across the United States: "Just say no."

That's the ultimate bottom line to all temptation, to "say no" to what is wrong in God's eyes.

When the urge comes to pick up that item in the department store and drop it into a purse or pocket and leave the store without paying for it, "Just say no" to that urge.

When the messages of television and movies say sex outside the bounds of marriage is acceptable and normal, and the opportunity presents itself for sexual behavior you know is wrong, "Just say no" to that desire.

When you don't know the answer and you have clear sight of the exam paper on the desk next to you, when you face the bottom line of the tax form and don't like the number you see, or when you are charged far below what you know to be the price and the opportunity to cheat is plainly yours, "Just say no" to that *opportunity*.

Some say "Just say no" is a good idea in theory, but it's very difficult in the reality of the moment.

We are called to recognize:

- *no person is beyond temptation.* If Jesus Christ, the Son of God, was tempted, you will be too! In what ways have you been tempted most often in the past? Did you ever reach a point where you thought you had fully conquered a particular temptation?

- *every person has a unique set of most enticing temptations.* Temptations are universal but people usually experience them very specifically and personally. What is a temptation to you may not be a temptation to another person. To know what is tempting can be a good starting point for knowing how to resist that temptation or avoid it. Do you know what is most tempting to you?

- *willpower isn't enough.* The problem with just saying "no" is that it relies solely on human willpower. Everyone eventually reaches a limit to his or her willpower. Are you routinely asking God to help you avoid temptation or to withstand it? Do you ask for God's help when you first feel temptation or when you are on the brink of giving in to temptation?

S
Supplementary Scriptures to Consider

When it comes to temptation, we are wise to recall the way Eve was tempted in the Garden of Eden:

> Now the serpent was more cunning than any beast of the field which the LORD God had made. And he said to the woman, "Has God indeed said, 'You shall not eat of every tree of the garden?'"
>
> And the woman said to the serpent, "We may eat the fruit of the trees of the garden; but of the fruit of the tree which is in the midst of the garden, God has said, 'You shall not eat it, nor shall you touch it, lest you die.'"
>
> Then the serpent said to the woman, "You will not surely die. For God knows that in the day you eat of it your eyes will be opened, and you will be like God, knowing good and evil."
>
> So when the woman saw that the tree was good for food, that it was pleasant to the eyes, and a tree desirable to make one wise, she took of its fruit and ate. She also gave to her husband with her, and he ate. Then the eyes of both of them were opened, and they knew that they were naked; and they sewed fig leaves together and made themselves coverings (Genesis 3:1–7).

• How is the serpent described? Is the devil any less cunning today? *He* knows your point of greatest weakness. Do *you*?

• The serpent questioned what God had said. He planted a seed of doubt. Consider a particular weakness you know you have. In what ways do you attempt to justify your partaking or participating in that sin as being OK? Are your justifications a form of doubt?

• Eve noted that the tree was good for food, beautiful to behold, and the key to being wise. All of these seemed like tremendous benefits if one could just overlook the death penalty associated with eating the fruit. In what ways does the devil always make sin look like a good thing? In what ways might Jesus have concluded that always having a ready source of food (there are a lot of rocks in Israel), having an immediate surge of notoriety and fame, and having rule over the kingdoms of the world would be *good* things for winning the world back to a full relationship with God the Father? In what ways does the devil try to make you think that a particular activity, substance, or relationship is going to be beneficial to you, perhaps even to your ministry or mission as a Christian?

• Eve never stopped to ask, "How much do I need to eat for all these good
benefits to be mine?" Nourishment and wisdom in just one bite? The
devil often tempts us with the easy way, the quick scheme, the overnight
success. Have you ever been tempted to take a short cut to a desirable
goal? What was the result?

• Eve shared the fruit with Adam. In what ways do we seek to involve
others in our sin? Why? With what results?

• Eve could have withstood the temptations of the serpent by simply
saying, "God said no." Jesus took this approach in the wilderness: "It is
written . . ." In other words, God has said no. How might this approach
work in your life when you face temptation?

James wrote to the early Christians:

Submit to God. Resist the devil and he will flee from you (James 4:7).

- What is the prerequisite—the prior step—to resisting the devil? In what ways do we *submit to God*?

- How does a person *resist the devil*? Jesus said to the tempter: "Away with you." What do you say when the devil speaks his lies and tempting words to your mind?

After forty days of no food, Jesus was weak physically. He was alone, in a naturally hostile physical environment. The devil was patient, waiting for that moment.

The Gospel of Matthew tells us

When He had fasted forty days and forty nights, afterward He was hungry. Now when the tempter came to Him . . .
(Matthew 4:2).

Do you find you are most likely to experience temptation when you are physically hungry, lonely, or overly tired? How does the devil play upon a person's lack in the temptation process? What might you do to make certain that you sustain a level of physical and emotional energy as a means of withstanding temptation? How important is it to stay in close association with other believers as a means of withstanding temptation?

I
Introspection and Implications

1. How do you feel after you give in to temptation? How important is it to go to God immediately and ask for forgiveness and help?

2. How do you feel after you have withstood a tempting thought or impulse? How important is it to immediately thank and praise God for His help? How dangerous is it to assume that you have withstood a temptation totally on your own strength or willpower?

3. What have you personally learned through years of being tempted and either giving in to temptation or successfully withstanding it? If you were to boil those lessons down to the "Top three things I've learned about temptation," what would those lessons be?

4. To what extent do you find yourself comparing your behavior to the behavior of others and concluding, "Other people seem to be able to get away with doing that, even though God says it is sin. It isn't fair!" Does any person ever truly get away with sinning?

5. How do you believe Jesus, in His humanity, was prepared more fully for ministry by overcoming the tempter in the wilderness? Do you believe it is possible that the Lord is preparing you for a greater ministry by allowing you to experience a particular season of temptation?

C

Communicating the Good News

Surely the good news of Jesus' temptation in the wilderness is this: We *can* defeat the devil. We do this by believing the Word of God and speaking it to the tempter every time he comes our way. However, what is the prerequisite? It is *knowing* the Word of God so you can use it as an arsenal of truth against the devil. What are the verses you would identify as "Away from me!" verses you might use in resisting the devil? What are verses you would teach to another believer to create an arsenal of truth in resisting the devil?

Many people today believe they simply cannot resist temptation. Others believe God has created within them certain weaknesses or propensities to sin. What do you say to a person who holds to such a belief? What hope can you give a person based upon the example of Jesus dealing with the tempter in the wilderness?

LESSON #3

JESUS TAUGHT HOW TO LIVE A BLESSED LIFE

Blessed: to experience an outpouring of goodness bestowed by God

B
Bible Focus

*And seeing the multitudes, He went up on a mountain, and
when He was seated His disciples came to Him. Then He
opened His mouth and taught them, saying,*
Blessed are the poor in spirit,
    For theirs is the kingdom of heaven.
Blessed are those who mourn,
    For they shall be comforted.
Blessed are the meek,
    For they shall inherit the earth.
Blessed are those who hunger and thirst for righteousness,
    For they shall be filled.
Blessed are the merciful,
    For they shall obtain mercy.
Blessed are the pure in heart,
    For they shall see God.
Blessed are the peacemakers,
    For they shall be called sons of God.
Blessed are those who are persecuted for righteousness' sake,
    For theirs is the kingdom of heaven.
*Blessed are you when they revile and persecute you, and say
all kinds of evil against you falsely for My sake. Rejoice and
be exceedingly glad, for great is your reward in heaven, for so
they persecuted the prophets who were before you (Matthew
5:1–12).*

This passage of Scripture is often called the Beatitudes, based on the word
blessed. It begins a section of the Gospel of Matthew commonly called the
Sermon on the Mount, based on the opening sentence that Jesus went up on a
mountain, sat down, and began to speak. This sermon, however, was likely a
composite of what Jesus preached repeatedly in His early months of ministry.
It was typical for rabbis in the time of Jesus to sit when they taught and to
engage their audiences— both small and large—in interactive questions and
answers. They often taught concepts repeatedly since their audience tended to
be different each time. Few people could take consecutive days from their
work to follow a rabbi. Most people who heard Jesus teach probably heard
Him only once or twice. The core concepts of Jesus' teaching, however,
became foundational to those who followed Him with regularity, and
Matthew—as a disciple of Jesus—very likely recorded what he perceived to be
Jesus' main concepts in the order of their importance or frequency of teaching.

The word *blessed* means *happy* or *fortunate* as a result of divine favor. The Jewish people at the time of Jesus were no different than people today. They wanted to be blessed! Their lives, however, tended to be extremely difficult—most lived from hand to mouth on the brink of poverty, and they experienced repression and opposition on all fronts as a nation occupied by Rome. If you had asked most of the people who came to hear Jesus teach, "Are you blessed?" their initial response would likely have been "No."

Also like many people today, the Jewish people in Jesus' time tended to perceive blessing in terms of material well-being, good health, and peaceful family relationships. This description of blessing was in keeping with various teachings from the Law of Moses that described a life of prosperity and wholeness for those who were to enter the Promised Land. Jesus turned this concept of blessing into an inner richness of spirit, which was possible to experience even in the midst of external poverty and distress. In Jesus' terms, to be *blessed* was to have a relationship with God, who satisfies the soul fully, now and forever. Jesus did not teach "blessed *will be*" but rather, "blessed *are.*" Although no person can experience the fullness of wholeness and blessing in this earthly life, a life of blessing *can* begin now, grow and flourish, and culminate in future eternity.

Spiritual blessing flows generously and richly from heaven to earth, and it flows specifically to those who are in right position to receive spiritual blessing. A good metaphor might be this: Spiritual blessing is poured out from heaven's windows into a funnel that extends all the way to you as an individual. A person standing under the funnel receives God's blessing; the person standing apart from the funnel does not. How does a person put himself into position to receive God's blessing? The Scriptures tell us God blesses the person who has a heart for Him, a desire to know Him, and who is obedient to the Spirit of God.

The terms in this passage warrant careful definition. Jesus described as *blessed* those who:

- are *poor in spirit*—in other words, they know they need God and are apart from Him, but have a desire for Him

- *mourn*—those who are sorrowful in spirit, because they know they have sinned or have caused the Spirit of God to grieve on their behalf

- are *meek*—those who are humble and willing to be led by the Spirit of God

- *hunger and thirst for righteousness*—those who make being in right relationship with God a top priority

- are *merciful*—those who are quick to forgive and extend mercy to others

- are *pure in heart*—those who have a clear conscience and godly motives

- are *peacemakers*—those who seek to bring others into reconciliation with God the Father

- are *persecuted for righteousness' sake*—those who suffer because they are in right relationship with God and are living as God commands

When a person bears any of these characteristics, that person is in precisely the right position to receive God's outpouring of spiritual favor! In other words, the person who is poor in spirit is in exactly the right position to enter the kingdom of heaven. (Conversely, the person who feels no need for God and doesn't feel apart from God nor desires to know God, cannot and will not be a candidate for citizenship in the kingdom of heaven.) The person who mourns his sin is in precisely the right position to receive God's forgiveness and the comfort that comes when a person is freed from guilt and shame. (The person who feels no sorrow for his sin will not be open to receiving God's forgiveness or experience the tremendous freedom that forgiveness produces in the human heart.)

The good news of the blessed life was and is this: *All* people can be blessed! True blessing is not something that can be externally defined or materially measured. Blessing is not limited, nor is it reserved for only a select few. Rather, it is unlimited, spiritual in nature, and readily available. Further-more, the blessed life as Jesus taught allows a person to focus on things that are eternal and genuinely valuable and diminish a preoccupation with the outer trappings of wealth, fame, position, status, beauty, and other externals that are not eternal and ultimately fade away.

Are you blessed today? Do you want to experience greater blessing? It's possible!

A
Application for Today

In terms of sheer numbers, more Christians are being persecuted around the world today than ever before in history. Countless millions in China and India are forbidden to speak the name of Jesus openly or to gather for worship of Jesus as Savior and Lord. In nations under Islamic rule, worship of Jesus as God is considered illegal and subject to punishment. In nations that are largely Islamic but not governed by Islam, Christians may worship but not encourage others to convert to Christ, and Christians routinely are refused opportunity to repair their church facilities or expand them.

In other areas of the world—including the United States of America—pockets of persecution exist in many communities, in many organizations, and in the workplace as a whole. The persecution may not be a matter of life and death, but it exists nonetheless in the form of ridicule and rejection.

In His teaching about the blessed life, Jesus pointed toward two realities. First, persecution is to be expected. Certainly if a person desires God, mourns his sin, seeks to follow God's leading, makes right-standing with God a top priority, freely extends forgiveness and mercy to others, has a clear conscience and godly motives, and openly seeks to bring people into reconciliation with God, that person is going to stand out in the world. He will be living against the grain of the world's system and values. He *will* be subject to persecution.

Second, Jesus made it clear that the persecution that puts us in the right position to receive the kingdom of heaven is persecution *for righteousness' sake*. There's no reward for our own human failures, foibles, or law-breaking.

Jesus also pointed to a great promise: those who are persecuted for righteousness' sake are in *precisely* the right position to live as full citizens in the kingdom of heaven on this earth *and* to receive great reward in heaven. To be a citizen of the kingdom of heaven means to have open and free access to God the Father, to have an assurance that God is in control of all things at all times, and therefore, to have an internal wellspring of joy, peace, faith, and love that is inexhaustible and unexplainable.

How do you feel about the concept of persecution? Most people want to avoid it at all costs. No one who is psychologically and emotionally healthy seeks it out. Some say if you have sufficient faith, you will not experience persecution. Yet Jesus said it is inevitable to those who live a godly life, and that it bears great reward.

Do you follow Christ in a way you hope will limit your exposure to persecution? Do you live a life of abandon, trusting God completely to honor what you say and do to uplift the name of Jesus? How do you discern between doing something for righteousness sake and being prudent in your relationships with unbelievers?

S
Supplementary Scriptures to Consider

The Lord gave a tremendous command and promise to Abram, the father of all who have faith, including us as Christians today:

> Now the LORD had said to Abram:
> "Get out of your country,
> From your family
> And from your father's house,

To a land that I will show you.
I will make you a great nation;
I will bless you
And make your name great;
And you shall be a blessing.
I will bless those who bless you,
And I will curse him who curses you;
And in you all the families of the earth shall be blessed"
        (Genesis 12:1–3).

• In what ways in your personal life does the Lord require you to leave the world and follow Christ to experience His blessing?

• Abram was promised that his name would be *great*. What does it mean to you to have a good name? A great name?

• In what ways have you been blessed even as you bless others?

• Have you ever experienced a situation or time in which those who perse-cuted you seemed to have the tables turned on them for no explainable reason?

• In what ways do you find it challenging to bless people who are not part of your family, heritage, culture, nationality, or race?

One of the foremost passages in the Law of Moses about blessing is this:

> "Now it shall come to pass, if you diligently obey the voice of the LORD your God, to observe carefully all His command-ments which I command you today, that the LORD your God will set you high above all nations of the earth. And all these blessings shall come upon you and overtake you, because you obey the voice of the LORD your God:
>
> "Blessed shall you be in the city, and blessed shall you be in the country.
>
> "Blessed shall be the fruit of your body, the produce of your ground and the increase of your herds, the increase of your cattle, and the offspring of your flocks.
>
> "Blessed shall be your basket and your kneading bowl.
>
> "Blessed shall you be when you come in, and blessed shall you be when you go out.

"The LORD will cause your enemies who rise against you to be defeated before your face; they shall come out against you one way and flee before you seven ways.

"The LORD will command the blessing on you in your storehouses and in all to which you set your hand, and He will bless you in the land which the LORD your God is giving you.

"The LORD will establish you as a holy people to Himself, just as He has sworn to you, if you keep the commandments of the LORD your God and walk in His ways. Then all the peoples of the earth shall see that you are called by the name of the LORD, and they shall be afraid of you. And the LORD will grant you plenty of goods, in the fruit of your body, in the increase of your livestock, and in the produce of your ground, in the land of which the LORD swore to your fathers to give you. The LORD will open to you His good treasure, the heavens, to give the rain to your land in its season, and to bless all the work of your hand. You shall lend to many nations, but you shall not borrow. And the LORD will make you the head and not the tail; you shall be above only, and not be beneath, if you heed the commandments of the LORD your God, which I command you today, and are careful to observe them. So you shall not turn aside from any of the words which I command you this day, to the right or the left, to go after other gods to serve them (Deuteronomy 28:1–14).

• Moses gave these words of blessing to the children of Israel prior to their entering the Promised Land. He taught them how to experience a blessed life in that land. Jesus gave words about the blessed life in the context of entering the kingdom of heaven. How do the teachings of Jesus build upon, and even fulfill, these words of Moses?

• In what ways do both the blessings of Moses and the blessings of Jesus require obedience to the commands of God?

The apostle Paul wrote to the Corinthians:

> Blessed be the God and Father of our Lord Jesus Christ, the Father of mercies and God of all comfort, who comforts us in all our tribulation, that we may be able to comfort those who are in any trouble, with the comfort with which we ourselves are comforted by God. For as the sufferings of Christ abound in us, so our consolation also abounds through Christ. Now if we are afflicted, it is for your consolation and salvation, which is effective for enduring the same sufferings which we also suffer. Or if we are comforted, it is for your consolation and salvation. And our hope for you is steadfast, because we know that as you are partakers of the sufferings, so also you will partake of the consolation (2 Corinthians 1:3–7).

How does living a blessed life put you in a prime position for ministering to others the love and hope of God? To what extent is suffering and persecution a necessity to you becoming an effective minister to others who are suffering or experiencing persecution?

I
Introspection and Implications

1. Have you ever felt justified in having your own personal pity party perhaps in the aftermath of a disappointment, loss, or a time when things just didn't turn out the way you thought they should? Does a Christian truly have a right to a pity party? In what ways does Jesus challenge us in the Beatitudes to put our focus on the future, not the present or past?

2. Have you ever experienced persecution *for righteousness' sake*? What did you do?

3. How is feeling *poor in spirit* different than having low self-esteem?

4. How is mourning sin different from feeling regret about getting caught?

5. How difficult is it to be *meek*—totally submissive to the will of God—in a world that rewards people for boldness and advocates the philosophy of looking out for number one?

6. Have you ever had someone come to you hoping to comfort you during a time of persecution? Did it make a difference that the person had experienced persecution, or hadn't experienced persecution, in his own life?

7. To what extent do you personally *hunger and thirst* for righteousness?

C
Communicating the Good News

What would you say to a person who suggested to you that it is more important to get along with other people than to confront them with their need for reconciliation with God?

What would you say to a person who confided in you that he was feeling intense guilt or shame?

How do you deal with the normal discouragement that comes when you tell another person about Jesus as Savior and the person seems to reject not only your message, but you personally?

How difficult do you find it to *rejoice and be exceedingly glad* when other people revile and persecute you for your relationship with Christ Jesus?

What comfort do you have in knowing you are not isolated from other people who are also seeking to be in position to live a blessed life?

LESSON #4

JESUS EMPHASIZED THE INNER LIFE AND THE LAW OF LOVE

*Law: a rule of conduct that governs
all actions within a kingdom
Motivation: an incentive that activates behavior*

B
Bible Focus

> *"Do not think that I came to destroy the Law or the Prophets. I did not come to destroy but to fulfill."*
>
> *"You have heard that it was said to those of old, 'You shall not murder, and whoever murders will be in danger of the judgment.' But I say to you that whoever is angry with his brother without a cause shall be in danger of the judgment. . . .*
>
> *"You have heard that it was said to those of old, 'You shall not commit adultery.' But I say to you that whoever looks at a woman to lust for her has already committed adultery with her in his heart. . . .*
>
> *"Furthermore it has been said, 'Whoever divorces his wife, let him give her a certificate of divorce.' But I say to you that whoever divorces his wife for any reason except sexual immorality causes her to commit adultery; and whoever marries a woman who is divorced commits adultery.*
>
> *"Again you have head that it was said to those of old, 'You shall not swear falsely, but shall perform your oaths to the Lord.' But I say to you, do not swear at all: neither by heaven, for it is God's throne; nor by the earth, for it is His footstool; nor by Jerusalem, for it is the city of the great King. Nor shall you swear by your head, because you cannot make one hair white or black. But let your 'Yes' be 'Yes,' and your 'No,' 'No.' For whatever is more than these is from the evil one.*
>
> *"You have heard that it was said, 'An eye for an eye and a tooth for a tooth.' But I tell you not to resist an evil person. But whoever slaps you on your right cheek, turn the other to him also. If anyone wants to sue you and take away your tunic, let him have your cloak also. And whoever compels you to go one mile, go with him two. Give to him who asks you, and from him who wants to borrow from you do not turn away.*
>
> *"You have heard that it was said, 'You shall love your neighbor and hate your enemy.' But I say to you, love your enemies, bless those who curse you, do good to those who the you, and pray for those who spitefully use you and persecute you, that you may be sons of your Father in heaven"* (Matthew 5:17, 21–22, 27–28, 32–45).

The Law of Moses governed the life of the Jewish people first and foremost. The Law was the means by which good Jews judged behavior.

On the surface, a person reading these verses from the Gospel of Matthew might conclude: Jesus made things a lot more difficult! His law was a lot tougher to keep. That was not necessarily the case. Rather, Jesus was calling His followers to recognize and keep the *spirit* of the Law of Moses, not just the letter of the law. He also was confronting several extensions to the Law of Moses. Through the centuries, thousands of laws had been added to the Law of Moses in an attempt to interpret and apply the law. These additional laws were burdensome, and in some cases, contrary to the true intent of God's commandments.

Ultimately, however, Jesus' purpose was to institute a new perception of law that governed the kingdom of heaven. The kingdom of heaven has only one ultimate law: the law of love. As God loved His creation, so His creation was to love Him and love one another. A loving generosity of spirit is the supreme motivation for all godly words and deeds.

The scribes and Pharisees, the religious leaders of Jesus' day, were experts in judging external deeds. Very little attention was paid to the inner workings of the spirit. Jesus, in sharp contrast, taught that all outer behavior flows from internal motivations. What a man *is* in his heart becomes the foundation for what that man *does* in his speech and behavior. All actions begin with spiritual attitude and motivation—as examples, the origin of murder is anger in the heart, adultery begins as lust in the fantasy of the mind, and the root of divorce is hardness of heart and an attitude of fault-finding.

The Law of Moses allowed for retaliation and compensation in situations that involved willful injury—payment of *an eye for an eye and a tooth for a tooth* (Exodus 21:24; Leviticus 24:20; Deuteronomy 19:21). Jesus taught that retaliation and compensation can produce a cycle of vengeance that has no end. Rather than retaliate and compensate, seek loving reconciliation! Generosity in reconciliation can break a cycle of vengeance and produce genuine peace. The Law of Moses taught people to love their neighbors (see Leviticus 19:18). Jesus said, in essence, "See all people as your neighbors, even those who set themselves up to be your enemies." A pursuit of reconciliation, love, and peace begins in the heart of man and flows outward.

Jesus gave a simple three-fold profile of loving behavior: bless those who curse you (loving speech), do good to those who hate you (loving actions), pray for those who spitefully use you and persecute you (loving attitude of wanting God's best for the person). Such manifestations of love can turn an enemy into a friend.

Jesus challenged His followers to turn inward and to judge their own inner state *first*. Evaluate your own motives, your own attitudes, your own desires for vengeance, your own selfishness and self-justification. If a person has his *inner* life in proper order, then his *outer* behavior will not only fulfill the Law of Moses, but create the atmosphere necessary for his living in the fullness of the kingdom of heaven.

A

Application for Today

More incidences of open and armed conflict exist in our world today than at any other time in recorded history. Some of the conflicts have taken on the status of international war (or conflict). Some are internal battles within the confines of a national border. Some are tribal skirmishes, some involve religious or sectarian violence, and some are extended family feuds. We live in a dangerous, angry, terror-prone world.

We in the United States experience conflict in a variety of forms, from road rage to family abuse to court battles. We live in a highly litigious society that seems intent on discovering the cause of every problem, and placing a price tag on all forms of negative effect. Divorce is rampant. Crime rates are high.

At the core of conflict is a craving for personal recognition and justice. The human heart wants what it believes is rightfully its own. We are self-centered human beings.

All war and all conflict can be reduced to one simple concept: "Me first."

Jesus turned this concept inside out. He taught, "God first. As God loves us, we love others, even as we love ourselves." Peace and reconciliation—and true godly behavior—can be reduced to one simple concept in the kingdom of heaven: active love. Love in the kingdom of God is not a sentimental emotion. It is an active verb, a genuine change agent.

How much more difficult is it to get our inner life in order than to adjust our own outward behavior? How much more difficult is it to change our attitudes, beliefs, motivations, and feelings, than to adjust our manners, protocol, and external behavior?

How much more difficult is it to put someone else first? How difficult is it to express love when we feel rejected, insulted, bruised, hurt, injured, harmed, or maligned?

How much more difficult is it to love than to hate?

S

Supplementary Scriptures to Consider

Later in the Gospel of Matthew, Jesus had a brief conversation with religious leaders about love and the law:

> When the Pharisees heard that He had silenced the Sadducees, they gathered together. Then one of them, a lawyer, asked Him a question, testing Him, and saying, "Teacher, which is the great commandment in the law?"

Jesus said to him, "You shall love the LORD your God with all your heart, with all your soul, and with all your mind. This is the first and great commandment. And the second is like it: 'You shall love your neighbor as yourself.' On these two commandments hang all the Law and the Prophets" (Matthew 22:34–40; see also Deuteronomy 6:5 and Leviticus 19:18).

- How do you define *love for your neighbor*? How do you define *love for God*?

- Which is easier, to love God or to love your neighbor?

Jesus also gave this summary of the law of love, which He identified as the teaching at the heart of the Law and Prophets:

"Whatever you want men to do to you, do also to them, for this is the Law and the Prophets" (Matthew 7:12).

- What is it that you desire for other people to do to you, or for you? Is there something you specifically desire for one particular person to do for you? What is your challenge in putting yourself into position to receive this desire?

- How do you believe this verse relates to inner motivation, beyond outer deeds?

Jesus taught a very clear link between what a person *is* on the inside and what a person *does* or *says* on the outside:

"Beware of false prophets who come to you in sheep's clothing, but inwardly they are ravenous wolves. You will know them by their fruits. Do men gather grapes from thornbushes or figs from thistles? Even so, every good tree bears good fruit, but a bad tree bears bad fruit. A good tree cannot bear bad fruit, nor can a bad tree bear good fruit. Every tree that does not bear good fruit is cut down and thrown into the fire. Therefore by their fruits you will know them" (Matthew 7:15–20).

- Have you ever encountered a wolf in sheep's clothing? What was the outcome? What lesson did you learn?

- Is there any way to determine if a tree is good or bad apart from its fruit?

- The apostle Paul taught that the fruit of the Spirit is *love, joy, peace, longsuffering, kindness, goodness, faithfulness, gentleness, self-control* (Galatians 5:22). How does each of these inner character qualities manifest itself in outer deeds?

I
Introspection and Implications

1. When you look deep into your own heart, is there an issue that cries out for you to deal with it before it manifests itself into outward acts of anger or hatred? What might you do to experience healing of this hurt, wound, or injustice?

2. How difficult is it to keep a need for justice from turning into a desire for vengeance? What can a person do to seek resolution of a hurtful situation without seeking to inflict pain on another person or entity?

3. Have you experienced a situation in which you, or perhaps another person, had a hardness of heart that led to rejection or estrangement? What steps can be taken for a person to soften his or her own heart?

4. What is the balance between admiring the beauty or physical fitness of another person and lusting for that person sexually?

5. We have all heard the phrase, "Say what you mean and mean what you say." How difficult is it to do this? What is the consequence of a broken promise or an unfulfilled vow? Is there a difference—in final consequence—between *willfully* saying something we don't mean and *accidentally* saying something we don't mean?

6. What are some practical ways in which you might *do good* to someone today who has set himself up to be your enemy?

C
Communicating the Good News

Reflect on this statement: A genuine expression of selfless love is perhaps the greatest witness for Christ Jesus a person can make. In what ways might you show a genuine expression of selfless love to another person today?

What might you say to a person who comes to you spouting anger, intense criticism or disapproval of another person, or confiding lustful fantasies about a married person?

How do you define *godly love* to a person who has not experienced God's love and forgiveness? Is it possible for a person who has not experienced spiritual renewal to understand a purity of love that is not rooted in sexual love or emotional sentiment?

What is the most loving thing you can do to or for another person? (Be specific. Think in terms of one individual.)

Lesson #5

Jesus Taught His Followers How to Pray

Prayer: communicating with God

B
Bible Focus

> *When you pray, you shall not be like the hypocrites. For*
> *they love to pray standing in the synagogues and on the*
> *corners of the streets, that they may be seen by men. As-*
> *suredly, I say to you, they have their reward. But you, when*
> *you pray, go into your room, and when you have shut your*
> *door, pray to your Father who is in the secret place; and your*
> *Father who sees in secret will reward you openly. And when*
> *you pray, do not use vain repetitions as the heathen do. For*
> *they think that they will be heard for their many words.*
>
> *Therefore do not be like them. For your Father knows the*
> *things you need of before you ask Him. In this manner, there-*
> *fore, pray:*
>
> *Our Father in heaven,*
> *Hallowed be Your name.*
> *Your kingdom come.*
> *Your will be done*
> *On earth as it is in heaven.*
> *Give us this day our daily bread.*
> *And forgive us our debts,*
> *As we forgive our debtors.*
> *And do not lead us into temptation,*
> *But deliver us from the evil one.*
> *For Yours is the kingdom and the power and the glory*
> *forever. Amen (Matthew 6:5–13).*

Although other Gospel accounts refer to Jesus praying and to His teachings about prayer, the Gospel of Matthew gives us Jesus' most complete teachings on prayer. Several things about this passage were vitally important to the Jewish audience to whom Matthew was writing—and to us, today.

First, prayer in Jesus' time was often elaborate and public, usually in a synagogue or the temple. Prayer was not regarded primarily as private commu-nication, but rather, public discourse. Many prominent religious leaders in Jerusalem held to a practice of voicing fairly long repetitive prayers as they made their way to the temple, calling attention to their own piety and creating an illusion that the more words voiced, the more sincere and acceptable the prayer. This, of course, left the common man—and the person of few words— feeling inept, unacceptable, and estranged from God. Jesus confronted this religious practice head-on. He certainly was not opposed to praying in public, but rather, to using prayer as a means of gaining a spiritual stamp of public approval.

Second, Jesus taught His followers that prayer was private, personal, and heartfelt communication with God. The Jews did not address God directly as their heavenly Father, but often referred to Him as Creator, King of the Universe, the Most High, or Lord. *Our Father* was a new title Jesus used, who actually chose the term *Abba* to describe His relationship with God the Father. (*Abba* has been translated *Daddy*—an affectionate term for Father.)

Third, Jesus did not prescribe that His followers memorize the prayer He taught them, nor did He teach that they limit themselves to the model prayer He gave them. Rather, He taught that their prayers should include these aspects:

- *praise for the Father*—*hallowed* means to *make holy* or to recognize that God's name and identity is worthy of all honor and praise

- *a willingness to submit to the Father's will*—to seek that God's kingdom and God's will be very present realities in a person's life

- *a petition for God to provide all a person needs every hour or every day*—*daily bread* to the Jew meant all that was necessary for living a life of wholeness. Beyond physical bread, it included all that was necessary intellectually, emotionally, and spiritually.

- *a petition for forgiveness*—couched in terms of a person's willingness to live in a state of forgiveness with other people

- *a petition for protection against evil*—including an ability to withstand all temptation

The prayer is framed with the awareness that God is the Sovereign ruler of His kingdom and that all power and glory belong to Him now and forever.

To pray in this manner is to pray with an attitude of praise, submission, and total dependency on God. It is to pray with a desire to forgive others, and to turn away from evil and toward what is godly. Jesus was teaching His followers an attitude and atmosphere of prayer as much as He was teaching them an outline of specific content.

Prayer flows from the heart of man to the heart of God. It is an expression of *your* innermost desires, longings, needs, and praise. Jesus said elsewhere in Matthew: "Those things which proceed out of the mouth come from the heart" (Matthew 15:18).

There isn't anything you can't express to God, in your own words, at any time and in any place. God longs to hear the prayers of His people.

A
Application for Today

A person once was criticized for praying apart from a book of prayers and for praying in terms of *You* and *Yours* rather than *Thee*, *Thou*, and *Thine*. The critic said with a degree of disgust in his voice, "You pray as if you *know* God."

The person who had been praying replied, "I do."

Generally speaking, the better we know a person the easier we find it to communicate with that person, and the more likely for our communication to include terms of endearment, affection, or familiarity.

This is certainly *not* to say we should ever become so casual in our relationship with God our heavenly Father that we lose sight of His awesome and infinite nature. Jesus concluded His model prayer with a reminder that God owns all things, governs all things, and is due the honor and glory for all things and from all people. It is to say that we who know Jesus as Savior and Lord are in *personal* relationship with God the Father, and our relationship is one in which we can and should feel total transparency, vulnerability, and ease. We can trust God with all our feelings, longings, and desires. We can entrust to God all our pain and sorrow. We can ask God for complete forgiveness and a bestowal of all His blessings—the fullness of His provision, protection, and presence.

How do you pray? How does the way you pray reflect the relationship you have with your heavenly Father?

S
Supplementary Scriptures to Consider

Jesus was very well aware that Jews often prayed as a preface or conclusion to their making a charitable gift to the less fortunate. Jesus addressed this as part of His teaching about prayer:

> "Take heed that you do not do your charitable deeds before men, to be seen by them. Otherwise you have no reward from your Father in heaven. Therefore, when you do a charitable deed, do not sound a trumpet before you as the hypocrites do in the synagogues and in the streets, that they may have glory from men. Assuredly, I say to you, they have their reward. But when you do a charitable deed, do not let your left hand know what your right hand is doing, that your charitable deed may be in secret, and your Father who sees in secret will Himself reward you openly" (Matthew 6:1–4).

- These verses above immediately precede Jesus' teaching about prayer. Both charitable deeds and prayer are to be done *in secret*, according to Jesus. What does it mean to you to give secretly? What does is it mean to you to pray *to your Father who is in the secret place*?

- Why do people seem to want public recognition for their charitable gifts? Why do people seem to need public affirmation of their spiritual acceptability or spiritual status?

Jesus also recognized that prayer for many Jews was linked to fasting. Immediately following His teaching on prayer in the Gospel of Matthew, we find Jesus' teaching about fasting:

> "Moreover, when you fast, do not be like the hypocrites, with a sad countenance. For they disfigure their faces that they may appear to men to be fasting. Assuredly, I say to you, they have their reward. But you, when you fast, anoint your head and wash your face, so that you do not appear to men to be fasting, but to your Father who is in the secret place; and your Father who sees in secret will reward you openly" (Matthew 6:16–18).

- The literal Hebrew word for *fasting* means to *cover over*, as to cover the mouth and abstain from food. Fasting was considered a sign of mourning, as an act of personal or corporate repentance, and as a means of gaining God's attention on behalf of suffering or sickness. People often fasted in a time of critical decision making. Have you ever fasted and prayed? To what benefit?

- What happens when a person does anything that draws public attention? Why is it important *not* to draw public attention when a person is seeking spiritual outcome?

The Gospel of Matthew emphasizes that Jesus drew a very specific conclusion about the way we are to engage in charitable giving, prayer, and fasting: *"Your Father who sees in secret will Himself reward you openly"* (Matthew 6:4, 6, and 18).

- How do you respond to this truth of God's Word? In what ways do you feel challenged?

- What rewards do you believe your heavenly Father has for you as you pursue a life of secret charitable giving, consistent prayer, and purposeful fasting? How do you believe the Father desires for you to respond to His rewarding you openly?

I
Introspection and Implications

1. Using ten words or less, how would you describe your prayer life? Reflect on the words you have used. What do you believe to be the ideal words to describe a person's prayer life? In what ways do you feel challenged regarding prayer?

2. Jesus noted *"your Father knows the things you have need of before you ask Him"* (Matthew 6:8). Why, then, ask? Who is being informed if you aren't praying publicly and the Father already knows?

3. Can a person ever be too familiar with God? Can a person ever speak to God or about God in terms that are too casual? How so? What are the implications?

4. Is there an aspect of prayer you believe you need to reemphasize or to implement in your daily communication with your heavenly Father? (Consider these aspects of prayer: praise, voiced submission and dependency, petitions for provision, cleansing of sin, and protection)

5. Why do you engage in charitable deeds and giving? Why do you pray? Why do you fast? In what ways is Jesus once again challenging a person's inner motives and the need for developing an inner life of spiritual character?

6. In what ways might a person find it freeing to give, pray, and fast *secretly*?

7. What is the importance of giving, praying, and fasting *regularly*? Frequently?

C
Communicating the Good News

Many people today seem to believe if they just do enough good works, or just go to church often enough, and say enough prayers in church, they will make it to heaven and receive ample eternal reward. How do you respond to these opinions? How would you respond to a person who made direct statements to you conveying these beliefs?

Jesus taught that our heavenly Father *sees* what we give and how we fast, and *hears* what we pray. Our heavenly Father always hears our prayers and always sees the true intent of our hearts. In what ways is this comforting? In what ways is it convicting?

LESSON #6

JESUS TAUGHT IN PARABLES

Parable: a short illustration or story
intended to teach a spiritual lesson

B
Bible Focus

On the same day Jesus went out of the house and sat by the sea. And great multitudes were gathered together to Him, so that He got into a boat and sat; and the whole multitude stood on the shore.

Then He spoke many things to them in parables, saying, "Behold, a sower went out to sow. And as he sowed, some seed fell by the wayside; and the birds came and devoured them. Some fell on stony places, where they did not have much earth; and they immediately sprang up because they had no depth of earth. But when the sun was up they were scorched, and because they had no root they withered away. And some fell among thorns, and the thorns sprang up and choked them. But others fell on good ground and yielded a crop: some a hundredfold, some sixty, some thirty. He who has ears to hear, let him!"

And the disciples came and said to Him, "Why do You speak to them in parables?"

He answered and said to them, "Because it has been given to you to know the mysteries of the kingdom of heaven, but to them it has not been given. For whoever has, to him more will be given, and He will have an abundance; but whoever does not have, even what he has will be taken away from him. Therefore I speak to them in parables, because seeing they do not see, and hearing they do not hear, nor do they understand.

But blessed are your eyes for they see, and your ears for they hear; for assuredly, I say to you that many prophets and righteous men desired to see what you see, and did not see it, and to hear what you hear, and did not hear it.

Therefore hear the parable of the sower: When anyone hears the word of the kingdom, and does not understand it, then the wicked one comes and snatches away what was sown in his heart. This is he who received seed by the wayside. But he who received the seed on stony places, this is he who hears the word and immediately receives it with joy; yet he has no root in himself, but endures only for a while. For when tribulation or persecution arises because of the word, immediately he stumbles. Now he who received seed among the thorns is he who hears the word, and the cares of this world and the deceitfulness of riches choke the word, and he becomes *unfruitful. But he who received seed on the good grounds is he who hears the word and understands it, who indeed bears fruit and produces: some a hundredfold, some sixty, some thirty" (Matthew 13:1–13, 16–23).*

Upon first reading these words of Jesus, a person may be tempted to conclude that Jesus was being very exclusive! He didn't expect everyone to understand what He taught. To the contrary, Jesus was an equal-opportunity teacher. He did not change His message from one audience to the next. Rather, He taught truth and lived truth. He knew realistically that not everyone was going to receive what He had to say, believe it, or follow through in applying His words to their lives.

Jesus' purpose was to begin conversation, and in so doing, to begin a process of seeking, asking, and learning. He knew that *only* what took root deep within a person, at the person's own volition and acceptance, would change a person's life. Again, it was a matter of people developing spiritual character and understanding from the inside out.

When a person hears a direct statement of admonition or advice, his response is intuitively and subconsciously to say "Yes" or "No" to the statement—either to take the statement as truth and perhaps agree to the point of positive action, or to dismiss the statement as unimportant and perhaps disagree to the point of taking opposite action. When a person hears a parable, however, the response is generally, "What does that story mean?" And more specifically, "What might that story mean to my life today?"

The amazing thing about the parables of Jesus is they hold layer upon layer of meaning for the person who will ask these questions. The parables of Jesus can be understood in a variety of ways, and they can be applied to a wide variety of situations in life. They hold meaning for and give guidance to the immature believer who may be encountering the parable for the first time, and also hold meaning for and give guidance to the mature believer who may be encountering the parable for the hundredth time. Jesus made this very clear in His Parable of the Sower.

The Sower, of course, is God the Father, and also God the Son, Jesus Himself. The Sower sows liberally and in an ongoing way. Jesus taught freely, openly, generously, and routinely. Some who came to hear Him came in opposition and with an attitude of skepticism or ridicule. Some came out of curiosity and no real desire to take what Jesus said to heart. Some responded favorably to what they heard, but didn't allow the truth of His words to sink deep in their spirits, take root, and bear fruit. Some came with truly open hearts and minds, and they were the ones who gained the most—they heard the truth, believed the truth, and began to live according to the truth. Their lives became spiritually fruitful according to the degree that they heard and applied the truth to their daily lives.

It is important to note that Jesus taught in parables to the masses, or to groups of people. He explained His parables to those who were His close followers. His communication one-to-one and in small groups was very different than His public discourse—He did not speak in parables to His closest followers, but rather, He spoke directly and concretely.

The question that confronts us all in the Parable of the Sower is this: "What type of soil am I?"

When you hear or read the Word of God, do you immediately seek to understand it more fully? Are you looking for meaning, perhaps something in the passage you've never seen before? Are you open to learning from God's Word and being changed by it? Are you looking for ways to apply God's Word and become a living example of God's Word in action?

Jesus cited the prophet Isaiah, saying, "Their ears are hard of hearing, and their eyes they have closed, lest they should see with their eyes and hear with their ears, lest they should understand with their hearts and turn, so that I should heal them" (Matthew 13:15; see Isaiah 6:9–10).

Jesus' desire is that we *want* to hear and understand so we might be changed and made whole.

A
Application for Today

Have you ever met a person you would describe as a know-it-all? How did you feel about this person? Did you enjoy listening to what that person had to say? Did you automatically put up barriers of resistance?

Conversely, have you ever met a teacher who spoke in such an engaging way that you clung to their every word? Did you want to take every course the person taught?

Attitude has a tremendous impact on how we learn and the degree to which we learn.

The same is true for the way we teach others—whether our students are our children, a Sunday school class, a church group or Bible study, a new employee at work, or young people in a club we are helping sponsor or lead. The old adage of communication is still true: Know your audience. Engage your audience. Communication is in the ears of the listener.

How often do we present the gospel in terms that are not understandable to a person who has never heard about Jesus? In truth, we all can do better in our communication of God's love and the truth Jesus Christ taught. We can learn a great deal from the *way* Jesus taught, in addition to learning from *what* He taught.

How often do we close our minds to a sermon because it seems to fly right over our heads or seems so simplistic that we conclude, "I know all this." In truth, we can learn something from every person, no matter the quality of the communication—something to do, something not to do, something worth believing, something requiring rejection. We learn most from observing and listening, yet few of us develop keen listening and observational skills.

How might you become a better listener?

How might you become a better observer?

How are good listening and good observation critical to spiritual discernment?

How might you become a better communicator?

How might you become a more empathetic teacher?

How is good and empathetic communication vital to having a positive witness for Christ Jesus?

S
Supplementary Scriptures to Consider

Jesus taught that there is tremendous benefit in acquiring the treasure of God's spiritual gifts and blessing:

> "Do not lay up for yourselves treasures on earth, where moth and rust destroy and where thieves break in and steal; but lay up for yourselves treasures in heaven, where neither moth nor rust destroys and where thieves do not break in and steal. For where your treasure is, there your heart will be also" (Matthew 6:19–21).

• What we know deep within can never be snatched from us—as the birds snatch the seed (the truth) in the Parable of the Sower. What we know deep within and apply daily does not wither. How can we make sure we allow God's Word to sink deep into our innermost spirit? What keys have you discovered for applying God's Word in direct and immediate ways to your practical daily circumstances and personal relationships?

• In what ways is truth a treasure that continues to yield good things to your life? Can you cite a specific truth you know today with even greater certainty than you knew it years ago? How much more today do you rely on those things you know with absolute assurance?

• How much do you value learning God's Word? How much do you value growing spiritually? How important is spending time each day reading your Bible?

Jesus said this about the learning process that produces spiritual maturity:

> "Ask, and it shall be given to you; seek, and you will find; knock, and it will be opened to you. For everyone who asks receives, and he who seeks finds, and to him who knocks it will be opened. Or what man is there among you who, if his son asks for bread will give him a stone? Or if he asks for a fish, will he give him a serpent? If you then, being evil, know how to give good gifts to your children, how much more will your Father who is in heaven give good things to those who ask Him! (Matthew 7:7–11)

• The words *ask*, *seek*, and *knock* in these verses—in the original language in which this was written—are better translated *ask, and keep on asking*;

seek, and keep on seeking; and *knock, and keep on knocking.* We must never think we know everything God desires for us to know—there's always more! What is it today about your life in Christ Jesus that you would like to know more about? How might you go about gaining that understanding?

• The words *receive, find,* and *be opened* are also better translated *receive, and keep on receiving*; *find, and keep on finding*; and *be opened, and keep on being opened.* The more we ask in an ongoing way, the more God answers us! What we ask as a young child will be different than what we ask as a young adult, which in turn will be different than what we ask as an elderly person. In like manner, we mature spiritually and our understanding grows deeper and deeper as long as we keep on asking, seeking, and knocking. God imparts His presence and His insight in increasing ways according to our capacity to receive, our ability to use what we find, and our ability to delight in what is opened to us. Reflect on your own faith journey. What issues were important to you years ago that are now resolved? How does this give you hope for your own spiritual growth ahead?

Jesus taught that we must learn before we teach!

"Why do you look at the speck in your brother's eye, but do not consider the plank in your own eye? Or how can you say to your brother, 'Let me remove the speck from your eye'; and look, a plank is in your own eye? Hypocrite! First, remove the

plank from your own eye, and then you will see clearly to
remove the speck from your brother's eye" (Matthew 7:3–5).

• What danger lies in attempting to teach something we don't truly know or
understand? What danger lies in giving advice we have never personally
lived out or put to the test?

• Why do we seem to be able to see error in others but not in ourselves?
Why do we need to surround ourselves with mature believers who can
teach us—in word and example—the Christian life?

I
Introspection and Implications

1. Have you ever found yourself saying as you read the Bible, "I just don't
understand this?" What might you do to gain understanding?

2. One of the most effective ways to ask questions is to ask yes or no questions.
   Is this true? Yes or no? Is this what I should do? Yes or no? Is this how I should act? Yes or no? What question do you desire for God to answer? How might you frame that question in a yes or no format?

3. What a person needs is generally what that person will seek, either consciously or subconsciously. What is it *you* need—emotionally, spiritually, relationally, materially?

4. One of the foremost ways God meets our needs—apart from the assurance of His presence with us always—is to give us an opportunity to give a little of the very thing we need. Need friendship? Give friendship! Need to feel valuable? Make another person feel valuable. Need a job? Volunteer and give your time and energy to someone who needs help. What opportunities is the Lord presenting to you to give?

5. We knock on doors to gain entrance and be closer to someone who is presently behind a closed door. We knock on doors spiritually to grow closer in our relationship to our heavenly Father. How do thanksgiving, praise, and adoration open up deeper intimacy with our Father? Can you cite an example of this in your own life?

C
Communicating the Good News

How important is it to speak personally to people in a way, and at a conceptual level, that they can comprehend what you are saying? Jesus taught that we are wise to speak to people what they are capable of receiving and believing, rather than moving beyond their maturity level to tell them what they are not yet capable of receiving or believing:

> "Do not give what is holy to the dogs; nor cast your pearls
> before swine, lest they trample them under their feet, and turn
> and tear you in pieces" (Matthew 7:6).

How might you discern the degree to which a person is receptive to what you have to say about the gospel?

How can you discern a person's level of understanding ?

The apostle Paul wrote to the Corinthians:

> When I was a child, I spoke as a child, I understood as a child,
> I thought as a child; but when I became a man, I put away
> childish things. For now we see in a mirror, dimly, but then
> face to face. Now I know in part, but then I shall know just as
> I also am known (1 Corinthians 13:11–12).

Reflect on one of the most sublime truths you know about Jesus Christ. How might you convey that truth to a five-year-old? To a brand new believer in Jesus?

In what ways does truth reveal to us who we *are* and challenge us to move toward what we might *become*? How might we apply this concept to our soul-winning efforts?

LESSON #7

JESUS TAUGHT ABOUT KINGDOM LIVING

*Kingdom living: understanding and
applying the principles and laws
of heaven to life on this earth. To seek
the kingdom of God is to abide with the King.
When we live in His presence and follow His
purposes, He takes responsibility for our needs.*

B
Bible Focus

Another parable He put forth to them, saying: "The kingdom of heaven is like a man who sowed good seed in his field; but while men slept, his enemy came and sowed tares among the heat and went his way. But when the grain had sprouted and produced a crop, then the tares also appeared. So the servants of the owner came and said to him, 'Sir, did you not sow good seed in your field? How then does it have tares?" He said to them, 'An enemy has done this.' The servants said to him, 'Do you want us then to go and gather them up?' But he said, 'No, lest while you gather up the tares you also uproot the wheat with them. Let both grow together until the harvest, and at the time of harvest I will say to the reapers, "First gather together the tares and bind them in bundles to burn them, but gather the wheat into my barn." '"

Another parable He put forth to them, saying, "The kingdom of heaven is like a mustard seed, which a man took and sowed in his field, which indeed is the least of all the seeds, but when it is grown it is greater than the herbs and becomes a tree, so that the birds of the air come and nest in its branches."

Another parable He spoke to them: "The kingdom of heaven is like leaven, which a woman took and hid in three measures of meal till it was all leavened."

"Again, the kingdom of heaven is like treasure hidden in a field, which a man found and hid; and for joy over it he goes and sells all that he has and buys that field.

"Again, the kingdom of heaven is like a merchant seeking beautiful pearls, who, when he had found one pearl of great price, went and sold all that he had and bought it.

"Again the kingdom of heaven of heaven is like a dragnet that was cast into the sea and gathered some of every kind, which, when it was full, they drew to shore; and they sat down and gathered the good into vessels, but threw the bad away. So it will be at the end of the age. The angels will come forth, separate the wicked from among the just, and cast them into the furnace of fire. There will be wailing and gnashing of teeth."

Jesus said to them, "Have you understood all these things?"

They said to Him, "Yes, Lord."
Then He said to them, "Therefore every scribe instructed
concerning the kingdom of heaven is like a householder who
brings out of his treasure things new and old" (Matthew
13:24–33, 44–52).

Jesus was not the first person in the Bible to tell parables. The Old Testament also has parables, and many of the messages from the prophets were couched in parable-like terms. One of Matthew's purposes in writing his Gospel is to show how Jesus filled the prophetic role of Messiah. He says about Jesus, "All these things Jesus spoke to the multitude in parables and without a parable He did not speak to them, that it might be fulfilled which was spoken by the prophet, saying: 'I will open My mouth in parables; I will utter things kept secret from the foundation of the world" (Matthew 13:34–35).

The prophets in the Old Testament called the people of God to righteous living—to actions in keeping with God's commandments, which put them into position to receive God's promises of blessing. Jesus called people to a right relationship with their heavenly Father—to live in a way that mirrored heaven's laws, and which put them in a position to receive all the spiritual blessings associated with the kingdom of heaven.

In Matthew 13, we find six parables specifically about the kingdom of heaven. Jesus makes it very clear that the kingdom of heaven . . .

- is established in the hearts of men and women in this world, but the final judgment regarding who is acceptable in the kingdom lies in the world to come; therefore, we must not judge too quickly who is *in* and who is *out*

- begins small in the human heart, but grows to the point of influencing others

- grows unseen in human hearts but is nevertheless expansive, just like leaven that is folded into dough

- brings great joy to the human spirit

- is valuable beyond anything else

- eventually becomes the criteria on which humanity is definitively judged. Those in the kingdom of heaven live eternally, those who are not in the kingdom do not.

Participation in the kingdom of heaven—and holding the spiritual treasure of the kingdom—is readily available to you, and to every person. But not all will choose to pursue the kingdom of heaven or attain its treasure. We each have a choice. The kingdom is not foisted on any person, it must be sought. Those who seek it, attain it by their faith.

For those who attain the kingdom of heaven, the reward is immeasurable. Are you living as a member of the kingdom of heaven?

A
Application for Today

Throughout the world, embassies are one of the most valuable political bridges among cultures and nations. A host nation grants property to a foreign entity, and that foreign entity sends ambassadors to the nation to be representative of the foreign nation's culture, laws, perspective, mores, and traditions. The embassy itself—the compound and its citizens—are not subject to the laws of the host nation, although they do their best to abide by the laws of the land whenever they find themselves outside the compound walls. The embassy is like a little bit of homeland planted on foreign soil.

So it is with us as followers of Christ Jesus. The apostle Paul referred to our being *ambassadors for Christ* (2 Corinthians 5:20). We are citizens of heaven from the moment we accept Jesus as Savior. We are subject to the laws of heaven. We are to live according to the principles of heaven. The Lord is our ultimate King. Our future home is heaven. We live now as strangers in an alien land.

It is because of this that we find ourselves *in* this world, but not truly *of* this world. Our deepest desire is to see God's will become the pervasive perspective and protocol of all human behavior. Our desire is to have all people experience a personal relationship with the Lord, and to give Him praise and homage at all times and in all things. Our desire is to live in peace with others and to see them grow into the fullness of Christ's character. We long to experience the fullness of love, joy, and peace that we know will one day be ours.

The parables of Jesus about the kingdom of heaven whet our appetite to experience that kingdom—as much as possible *now*, but most assuredly, *then*.

How much do you want the kingdom of heaven to be the way you live?

How much do you long to see others gain entrance into that kingdom?

What do you believe are your responsibilities as a citizen of the kingdom of heaven?

The answers to these questions determine to a great extent both your relationship with Christ Jesus and your desire to grow spiritually. The answers most certainly impact the degree to which you will seek to share the truth of Christ Jesus with others.

S
Supplementary Scriptures to Consider

Jesus placed the highest priority on entering into and experiencing the kingdom of heaven. He taught that pursuing the kingdom of God—and being in right relationship with God—was the key to living a life free of anxiety and the key to having all other needs in life met. He taught:

> "Therefore I say to you, do not worry about your life, what you will eat or what you will drink; nor about your body, what you will put on. Is not life more than food, and the body more than clothing? Look at the birds of the air, for they neither sow nor reap nor gather into barns; yet your heavenly Father feeds them. Are you not of more value than they? Which of you by worrying can add one cubit to his stature?
>
> "So why worry about clothing? Consider the lilies of the field, how they grow; they neither toil nor spin; and yet I say to you that even Solomon in all his glory was not arrayed like one of these. Now if God so clothes the grass of the field, which today is, and tomorrow is thrown into the oven, will He not much more clothe you, O you of little faith?
>
> "Therefore do not worry, saying, 'What shall we eat?' or 'What shall we drink?' or 'What shall we wear?' For after all these things the Gentiles seek. For your heavenly Father knows that you need all these things. But seek first the kingdom of God and His righteousness, and all these things shall be added to you. Therefore do not worry about tomorrow, for tomorrow will worry about its own things. Sufficient for the day is its own trouble" (Matthew 6:25–34).

- How difficult is it to live an anxiety-free life? How much of our stress and anxiety today involves striving for material goods and outward status or appearance?

- What does it mean to you to *seek first the kingdom of God*? How does this impact your overall priorities in life? Your daily schedule?

The Gospel of Matthew does not give us an elaborate explanation of all the parables Jesus taught. One parable that is given a full explanation, though, is the parable of the wheat and tares.

> He answered and said to them: "He who sows the good seed is the Son of Man. The field is the world, the good seeds are the sons of the kingdom, but the tares are the sons of the wicked one. The enemy who sowed them is the devil, the harvest is the end of the age, and the reapers are the angels. Therefore as the tares are gathered and burned in the fire, so it will be at the end of this age. The Son of Man will send out His angels, and they will gather out of His kingdom all things that offend, and those who practice lawlessness, and will cast them into the furnace of fire. There will be wailing and gnashing of teeth. Then the righteous will shine forth as the sun in the kingdom of their Father. He who has ears to hear let him hear"
> (Matthew 13:37–43).

- Many people today are uncomfortable with the concept of a final judgment that results in some people experiencing the *kingdom of their Father* and others a *furnace of fire*. Jesus clearly taught such a judgment, not only in this parable but elsewhere in the Gospel of Matthew. (See also the Parable of the Talents in Matthew 25:14–30 and the Judgment described in Matthew 22:31–46.) How do you respond to those who might say, "God would never send any person to hell? Everyone gets to heaven, just perhaps in different ways?"

- We live in a world that tends to evaluate people on a scale of goodness—some people live better lives than others. Jesus, however, divided people into two clearly-designated groups in this parable: the *sons of the kingdom* and the *sons of the wicked one*. What is the criterion for being in one group or the other?

- Jesus taught in this parable that people can choose to do what offends. To *practice lawlessness* implies willful behavior. How important is it that we give witness to the truth that a person can *choose* to follow Christ, and that every person is responsible for making a personal choice for Christ Jesus?

In the Gospel of Matthew, Jesus repeatedly holds out a challenge to His followers that they live in a way that inspires other people to enter into a deep and meaningful relationship with their heavenly Father, and to follow His commands. He taught:

> "You are the salt of the earth; but if the salt loses its flavor, how shall it be seasoned? It is then good for nothing but to be thrown out and trampled underfoot by men.
> "You are the light of the world. A city that is set on a hill cannot be hidden. Nor do they light a lamp and put it under basket, but on a lampstand, and it gives light to all who are in the house. Let your light so shine before men that they may see your good works and glorify your Father in heaven" (Matthew 5:13–16).

- What are the characteristics of salt that relate to your being a witness for Christ Jesus? (Note the only two ways salt can lose its flavor is for it to become so diluted with water, or become so polluted with dirt or other substances, that it ceases to be salty.) Can a person be too salty?

How do you season your life with truth in a way that compels another person to seek the kingdom of heaven? (Think specifically about one person.)

- What are the characteristics of light that relate to your being a witness for Christ Jesus?

I
Introspection and Implications

1. In what ways does seeking, or pursuing, the kingdom of heaven change a person's perspective on daily routines? In what ways does it shape a

person's goals? In what ways does it become a template for a person's planning?

2. To what degree do you value the kingdom of heaven? Jesus taught in one of His parables: "The kingdom of heaven is like treasure hidden in a field, which a man found and hid; and for joy over it he goes and sells all that he has and buys that field" (Matthew 13:44). Reflect on this parable and its application to your own life. Have you found the kingdom of heaven to be a genuine treasure? To what extent does your relationship with the Lord give you joy? To what extent does your living out the kingdom of heaven become not only a top priority, but your *only* priority?

3. Jesus never attempted to convince His followers that living out the kingdom of heaven on this earth was an easy task; rather, it was the only way to live that had bearing on eternity. He taught:

> "If anyone desires to come after Me, let him deny himself, and take up his cross, and follow Me. For whoever desires to save his life will lose it, but whoever loses his life for My sake will find it. For what profit is it to a man if he gains the whole world, and loses his own soul? Or what will a man give in exchange for his soul? For the Son of Man will come in the glory of His Father with His angels, and then He will reward each according to his works" (Matthew 16:24–27).

How do you respond to these words of Jesus? What does it mean for you to *deny yourself*? What does it mean for you to *take up* your own cross and follow Christ? What does it mean to *lose your life* for His sake?"

C
Communicating the Good News

Matthew ends his Gospel with a command for Jesus' followers to extend His message of the kingdom of heaven to all people:

> And Jesus came and spoke to them, saying, "All authority has been given to Me in heaven and on earth. Go therefore and make disciples of all the nations, baptizing them in the name of the Father and of the Son and of the Holy Spirit, teaching them to observe all things that I have commanded you; and lo, I am with you always, even to the end of the age" (Matthew 28:18–20).

What three things did Jesus command His followers, including us, to do?

What does it mean to *make disciples of all the nations*? How might we each do that more effectively?

What is associated with baptism? Consider what each of these concepts means: *confession, conversion, repentance, cleansing,* and *living in the identity of the name of the Father and of the Son and of the Holy Spirit.*

What does it mean to teach others to *observe* (not just *perceive* or *see*) what Jesus commanded?

What is Jesus' role in this partnership of evangelism?

How does knowing that Jesus gives us authority to be His witnesses, and that He is present with us always, give us confidence and courage to do our part?

NOTES TO LEADERS
OF SMALL GROUPS

A s the leader of a small discussion group, think of yourself as a facilitator with three main roles:

- Get the discussion started

- Involve every person in the group

- Encourage an open, candid discussion that remains focused on the Bible

You certainly don't need to be the person with all the answers! In truth, much of your role is to ask questions, such as:

- What impacted you most in this lesson?

- What part of the lesson did you find troubling?

- What part of the lesson was encouraging or insightful?

- What part of the lesson would you like to explore further?

Express to the group at the outset of your study that your goal as a group is to gain new insights into God's Word—this is not the forum for defending a point of doctrine or a theological opinion. Stay focused on what God's Word says and means. The purpose of the study is also to share insights of how to apply God's Word to everyday life. *Every* person in the group can and should contribute—the collective wisdom that flows from Bible-focused discussion is often very rich and deep.

Seek to create an environment in which every member of the group feels free to ask questions of other members to gain greater understanding. Encourage group members to voice their appreciation to one another for new insights gained, and to be supportive of one another personally. Take the lead in doing this. Genuinely appreciate and value the contributions each person makes.

You may want to begin each study by having one or more members of the group read through the section provided under "Bible Focus." Ask the group specifically if it desires to discuss any of the questions under the "Application for Today" section, the "Supplemental Scriptures to Consider" section, the "Introspection and Implications" and "Communicating the Good News" section. You do not need to come to a definitive conclusion or consensus about any question asked in this study. Rather, encourage your group if it does not have a satisfactory Bible-based answer to a question that the group engage in further asking, seeking, and knocking strategies to discover the answers. Remember the words of Jesus: "Ask, and it will be given to you; seek, and you will find; knock, and it will be opened to you. For everyone who asks receives, and he who seeks finds, and to him who knocks it will be opened" (Matthew 7:7–8).

Finally, open and close your study with prayer. Ask the Holy Spirit, whom Jesus called the Spirit of Truth, to guide your discussion and to reveal what is of eternal benefit to you individually and as a group. As you close your time together, ask the Holy Spirit to seal to your remembrance what you have read and studied, and to show you ways in the upcoming days, weeks, and months how to apply what you have studied to your daily life and relationships.

General Themes for the Lessons

Each lesson in this study has one or more core themes. Continually pull the group back to these themes. You can do this by asking simple questions, such as, "How does that relate to _____?", "How does that help us better understand the concept of _____?", or "In what ways does that help us apply the principle of _____?"

A summary of general themes or concepts in each lesson follows:

Lesson #1
JESUS IS KING!
Jesus' identity as the Christ, the Savior, the Messiah
Your identity as a believer in Christ Jesus
Having proof for what you believe and what you profess

Lesson #2

JESUS OVERCAME THE TEMPTER

Recognizing and overcoming temptation

Submission to God

Resisting the devil

Lesson #3

JESUS TAUGHT HOW TO LIVE A BLESSED LIFE

Blessing

Righteousness

Entering the kingdom of heaven

Placing priority on spiritual blessing

Lesson #4

JESUS EMPHASIZED THE INNER LIFE AND THE LAW OF LOVE

Behavior flows from inner character and identity

Inner motivations

Christ's law of love being pervasive in the kingdom of heaven

Integrity being total harmony between what a person says and does

Lesson #5

JESUS TAUGHT HIS FOLLOWERS HOW TO PRAY

The Model Prayer

Communicating with God

Prayer and charitable giving

Prayer and fasting

Rewards associated with prayer

Lesson #6

JESUS TAUGHT IN PARABLES

Growing into spiritual maturity

Learning spiritual principles

The processes of asking, seeking, and knocking

Lesson #7

JESUS TAUGHT ABOUT KINGDOM LIVING

Citizenship in the kingdom of heaven

Making the kingdom of heaven a priority and focus of life

Sharing the good news of the kingdom of heaven with others

The Great Commission

NOTES